DR. FERRIS W. CORBETT, DRPH

The Divine Mind: Understanding God Through the Lens of Neuroscience

Where Faith Meets Neural Networks: A Comprehensive Guide to Neurotheology

First edition

This book was professionally typeset on Reedsy.
Find out more at reedsy.com

Contents

Preface

There is a silent, intangible moment when a person reaches out in prayer, awe, desperation, or worship. The world quiets and something stirs in the soul. For centuries, this was solely the domain of faith. But today, science is listening, too.

This book was born from that intersection: where neurons fire and the Spirit moves, and where synapses and Scripture meet.

Neurotheology—a term that first gained traction in the 1990s. It is the study of the relationship between the brain and religious experience. It asks questions like:

- *What happens in the brain when someone prays?*
- *Can spiritual experiences be mapped neurologically?*
- *Are we biologically wired for belief?*
- *And if so, what does that say about God?*

Some worry this field threatens faith—as if putting God under a microscope reduces Him to biology. I do not see it that way. I see it as an invitation. If we are made in the image of God, then understanding how our minds work is, in a very real way, a kind of reverent exploration. It is asking, with curiosity and humility: *What has God built into the architecture of the human mind to help us find Him?*

The Divine Mind is not a book about choosing between faith or science. It is about refusing to choose. It is about looking at both the Bible and the brain scan and saying, "Yes, this too."

Throughout this book, we will explore how prayer shapes the brain, how trauma alters it, how deconstruction and doubt rewire belief systems—and how reconstruction heals them. We will examine what Scripture says about the mind and what neuroscience now confirms. We will look at worship, miracles, shame, community, consciousness, and the soul. And we will do it without flinching from mystery or ignoring data.

This is not a theology textbook. It is not a neuroscience manual. It is a guide for whole-person believers—those who want to love God not just with heart and soul, but with **all their mind** (Luke 10:27). For the skeptic, the deconstructing believer, the curious therapist, the open-minded pastor, and anyone who senses there is something sacred in our search for meaning.

You do not have to be a scientist to read this book. You do not have to be a theologian either. You just have to be willing to hold wonder in one hand and evidence in the other.

Let's begin.

Introduction

Bridging the Gap Between Faith and Science

We are living in a time when people are both leaving organized religion and searching for deeper meaning at unprecedented levels. Some walk away from faith because it no longer fits the world they live in. Others cling tightly, suspicious of anything "scientific" that might undermine their belief. Still others—perhaps the majority—are caught in the middle, asking: *Can I trust both my faith and my intellect?*

This book says: **yes.**

The Divine Mind is an exploration of how belief interacts with biology—how the brain processes faith, prayer, worship, and even doubt. But it is not a book trying to reduce God to neurons or dismiss the spiritual experience as an illusion. On the contrary, it is a search for understanding: What has God built into the brain that draws us toward Him?

The goal is simple and bold: to help readers—whether you are a believer, skeptic, or seeker—understand how neuroscience and faith can work together. To show that loving God with your **mind** (Luke 10:27) is not a metaphor. It is an invitation to wholeness.

Neurotheology is the lens we will use. It is an interdisciplinary field where theology and neuroscience intersect. It does not pretend to have every answer. But it does give us better questions. Questions like:

- *What is happening in the brain when someone prays?*
- *Why are humans wired for spiritual experience across cultures and centuries?*

- *How do trauma, community, and scripture affect brain development?*
- *Can understanding the brain help us better understand God—or at least how we seek Him?*

This book will not ask you to trade faith for science, or science for faith. It will ask you to consider that maybe both belong.

2. The Origins of Neurotheology: When and Why It Began

Neurotheology is a relatively new field, emerging in the late 20th century. Though humans have been having religious experiences for millennia, it was not until the 1990s that researchers began systematically exploring them using neuroscience.

The term "neurotheology" was coined and popularized by neuroscientist **Dr. Andrew Newberg** and psychiatrist/theologian **Eugene d'Aquili**. They asked a radical question: *What if we could observe the brain during a spiritual experience?*

So they did. Using SPECT and later fMRI imaging, they studied the brains of meditating monks, praying nuns, Pentecostal worshipers, and others in deep states of spiritual focus. What they found was not a "God spot" in the brain—but a complex network of regions involved in transcendent experience, selflessness, and emotional integration.

Their findings did not explain God away. Instead, they revealed that **our brains seem wired for the sacred.**

Why does that matter? Because it means the urge to seek, worship, and connect with something greater is not just learned. It is embedded. It is not evidence against God—it might be evidence of **how** God made us.

> ***"God did this so that they would seek him and perhaps reach out for him and find him, though he is not far from any one of us."*** **—Acts 17:27**
>
> ***"It is the glory of God to conceal a matter; to search out a matter is the glory of kings."*** **—Proverbs 25:2**

Science and theology are often treated as opposites. Neurotheology says they are partners in the same search: the human longing to understand why we are here, and who we belong to.

3. Why Neurotheology Matters Now

We are at a tipping point in culture. Here is why this matters more than ever:

- **The rise of the "nones"**—those with no religious affiliation—is growing fast. But many of these people are not atheists. They are spiritually open, just institutionally burned. Neurotheology offers a language for spiritual experience that does not rely on dogma but still respects depth.
- **Mental health crises** are exploding. Anxiety, depression, trauma, and loneliness are surging. Faith communities have long been places of healing, but often lack psychological tools. Neuroscience has tools but often lacks soul. Together, they can help people heal holistically.
- **Culture is hungry for integrated truth.** People are tired of either/or thinking. They want a worldview that holds both mystery and method, revelation and research. Neurotheology does not simplify the tension—it honors it.
- **Technology is reshaping human consciousness.** AI, social media, and neuro-enhancement are changing how we think, feel, and relate. If the church does not understand the brain, it will fall behind—and worse, it may misdiagnose what people need most. Faith must be both spiritually grounded and neurologically literate.

Reflection

How does understanding the brain help us seek God with more clarity, humility, and depth?

What if the science of the mind did not challenge your faith, but matured it?

If God created the heavens and the earth—and the neurons that perceive them—then exploring the brain is not a detour from discipleship. It might be part of it.

Let's begin the journey.

1

Chapter 1: The Brain That Believes – A Foundation for Neurotheology

1.1 The Biology of Belief

Faith is not just a philosophical or theological concept—it is also a neurological experience. When someone prays, worships, meditates, or contemplates the divine, the brain is not passive. It lights up.

The primary regions involved in spiritual experiences are:

- **Prefrontal Cortex** – Associated with attention, planning, self-reflection, and moral reasoning. During prayer or meditation, this area often shows increased activity. It is where focus sharpens and moral convictions are processed.
- **Temporal Lobes** – Key in processing language, emotion, and memory. They are especially active during religious experiences and are involved in the perception of meaning and connection—whether to others, to Scripture, or to God.
- **Limbic System** – Including the amygdala and hippocampus, it governs emotion and memory. It plays a central role in feelings of awe, love, fear,

and transcendence—core elements of most religious traditions.

These are not isolated systems. They work together. For example, when someone sings a worship song, the prefrontal cortex processes the lyrics' meaning, the limbic system reacts emotionally, and the motor cortex may activate through movement or dance. The whole brain is engaged.

At the biochemical level, **neurotransmitters** are the messengers. During spiritual experiences:

- **Dopamine** (pleasure and reward) surges during moments of joy or connection to God.
- **Serotonin** (mood regulation) may increase during practices like prayer or gratitude, contributing to inner peace.
- **Oxytocin** (bonding and trust) is released during communal worship and shared faith rituals, deepening relational ties.
- **GABA** (a calming neurotransmitter) rises in contemplative practices, reducing anxiety and helping the mind enter peaceful states.

Spirituality is not an abstract concept floating above the brain—it is something deeply embedded **within it**.

1.2 The God Module: Myth or Mechanism?

One of the most publicized—and misunderstood—concepts in neurotheology is the idea of a "**God spot**" in the brain. This idea suggests that there is a specific region responsible for belief in God as if faith could be boiled down to a single circuit.

This came from early studies in the 1990s that observed unusual religious experiences in people with activity in the **temporal lobes**, particularly those with **temporal lobe epilepsy (TLE)**. Some of these individuals reported intense spiritual visions, voices, or a feeling of divine presence. Researchers like Dr. V.S. Ramachandran proposed that the temporal lobe could house a "God module."

However, more recent research shows that **no single "God spot" exists**. Instead, spiritual experience activates a **network** of regions throughout the brain. These include areas involved in attention, emotion, sensory perception, and social connection.

Still, the connection between **temporal lobe activity and spiritual intensity** remains compelling. It raises important questions:

- Are some people more neurologically predisposed to spiritual experiences?
- Do mystical experiences arise from neurological irregularities—or do they point to a deeper spiritual reality?

Rather than using neuroscience to explain faith away, we can frame it like this: **the brain is the organ of spiritual experience**, just as the eye is the organ of sight. It does not mean what you see is not real—it means your body is equipped to see it.

1.3 Faith and Brain Development

Belief does not develop in a vacuum—it is shaped by biology, experience, culture, and age. Neuroscience shows that **religious belief changes across the lifespan**, and that early spiritual exposure influences how the brain develops.

In childhood, the brain is highly plastic—constantly forming and pruning connections based on experience. Religious rituals, stories, and relationships experienced early in life can shape how the brain processes morality, trust, and purpose.

Studies show that:

- **Children raised in religious environments** often show stronger development in areas tied to empathy, emotional regulation, and delayed gratification.
- **Adolescents** who internalize faith practices tend to have more resilience against depression and anxiety, likely due to increased meaning-making

and community bonding.

- In **adulthood**, spiritual beliefs can reinforce neural circuits related to habit, identity, and worldview. Belief systems become more stable, though still open to transformation—especially through trauma, crisis, or significant life events.
- **Older adults** often experience a deepening of spiritual experience, and prayer or meditation can slow cognitive decline and reduce stress-related inflammation in the brain.

This aligns with biblical themes of **formation** over time. As Paul writes in *Romans 12:2:*

> "Be transformed by the renewing of your mind."

Faith is not static. It evolves. It grows—or decays—depending on what the brain is exposed to, and what practices shape it. The good news? The brain's plasticity means belief can be **renewed** at any age.

Reflection

> "I will praise You because I am fearfully and wonderfully made." — Psalm 139:14

You are not just a soul floating in a body. You are a mind-body-soul being, wired by God for connection, meaning, and transcendence.

To worship with all your mind is not just poetic—it is neurobiological. You are using the very structures and chemicals of your brain to reach toward the divine. And that is not accidental.

So the question becomes:

What does it mean to worship with both brain and spirit?

What does it look like to engage God with the whole self—not just emotionally or intellectually, but physiologically?

This is the foundation of neurotheology. The study of the brain does not threaten the sacred—it reveals how deeply the sacred is built into the brain.

Let's keep going.

2

Chapter 2: Scripture and Synapses – How the Bible Speaks to the Brain

2.1 The Word and the Wiring

Long before we understood neuroplasticity or synaptic pathways, Scripture described what we now know to be scientifically true: **what you meditate on shapes your mind**.

> "Blessed is the one... whose delight is in the law of the Lord, and who meditates on his law day and night." — Psalm 1:1–2

Meditation in biblical terms is not emptying the mind—it is filling it. Slowly, repeatedly, intentionally. The Hebrew word *hagah*, translated "meditate," also means to mutter, murmur, repeat under the breath. This repetition—what today we might call *active recall* or *mental rehearsal*—has profound neurological effects.

Modern neuroscience confirms that when we engage in repetitive practices like scripture reading, **neural pathways are strengthened**. Like walking a path through a forest again and again, the more a thought is activated, the more accessible and automatic it becomes.

When believers internalize Scripture, it begins to rewire their **default mode network**—the brain's system for self-referential thinking. In other words, **how we think about ourselves, others, and God** is directly affected by what we consistently meditate on.

- Reading "You are fearfully and wonderfully made" (Psalm 139:14) consistently can reframe self-worth.
- Meditating on "Perfect love casts out fear" (1 John 4:18) can dampen anxiety circuits over time.
- Rehearsing "Love is patient, love is kind..." (1 Corinthians 13) can recondition relational responses.

The Bible is not just read with the eyes. It is encoded, stored, and activated in the **neural networks of the brain**. And those networks shape who we become.

2.2 Neuroplasticity and Transformation

> "Do not conform to the pattern of this world, but be transformed by the renewing of your mind." — Romans 12:2

Paul did not need an fMRI to know that transformation happens in the mind—but modern neuroscience shows us just how accurate this was.

Neuroplasticity is the brain's ability to change itself. Every thought, behavior, emotion, and habit we practice actually **reshapes the brain's structure**. New neural pathways form. Old ones weaken or vanish. What you think about—especially with focus and repetition—becomes easier to think about again.

This is the foundation of:

- **Cognitive Behavioral Therapy (CBT)** — changing thought patterns to change emotional and behavioral responses.
- **Habit formation science** — using cues, routines, and rewards to rewire behavioral loops.

- **Mindfulness training** — observing thought patterns to gain control over them.

Scripture aligns with all of these. Take the process of renewal Paul describes:

1. **Refuse to conform** – recognize unhealthy patterns
2. **Be transformed** – invite new ways of thinking
3. **Renew your mind** – make it an ongoing process

When you align your daily habits with Scripture—reading it, memorizing it, applying it—you are participating in literal **brain change**. The Spirit does the internal work, but it often flows through the neurological systems God designed.

This is not about behavior modification. It is about **identity transformation** at the neural level. The gospel does not just ask for belief—it offers renewal. And the brain is the instrument through which that renewal unfolds.

2.3 Memory, Trauma, and Redemption

Many people carry pain in both spirit and brain. Traumatic memories are stored not only in our emotions but in the very wiring of our **limbic system** and **amygdala**—the parts of the brain responsible for fear, survival, and emotional processing.

Here is where Scripture becomes more than information—it becomes intervention.

When traumatic memories are triggered, the brain reverts to survival mode. But when a person has internalized Scripture, **those words can act as anchors**, calming the nervous system, reframing the moment, and guiding the person back to safety.

- "Even though I walk through the valley... I will fear no evil" (Psalm 23:4)
- "The Lord is close to the brokenhearted" (Psalm 34:18)
- "Cast all your anxiety on Him..." (1 Peter 5:7)

Neuroscience calls this **memory reconsolidation**—the process by which painful memories can be reinterpreted and reduced in emotional intensity by attaching new meaning. In faith terms, we might call this **redemption**.

Even more powerful is the role of **scripture memory**. When a verse is embedded in long-term memory, it becomes neurologically accessible during high-stress moments. It is not abstract—it is instinctive.

Practices like **Lectio Divina**, **breath prayers**, and **guided Scripture meditation** have been shown to reduce stress, regulate cortisol levels, and increase feelings of hope and security. This is not self-help. It is spirit-and-brain-level healing.

Scripture speaks to trauma not with clichés, but with **neural possibility**—that what was once wired in pain can, through grace and practice, be rewired in peace.

Reflection

> "For the word of God is living and active. Sharper than any double-edged sword... it judges the thoughts and attitudes of the heart." — Hebrews 4:12

When you read Scripture, you are not just consuming truth. Your brain is being shaped by it. Your neurons fire, your networks respond, and your identity recalibrates.

You are literally *being renewed.*

So ask yourself:

- What scriptures are shaping my neural pathways?
- What thoughts are becoming automatic—and are they aligned with truth?
- What does my brain do with the Word of God, and what does God do with my brain through His Word?

This is not a metaphor. It is reality. You are fearfully and wonderfully made—and the Word is alive in the system He made.

3

Chapter 3: Prayer and the Neural Pathways of Presence

Prayer is one of the most personal, profound, and mysterious aspects of faith. It is also one of the most neurologically active.

Whether whispered in desperation, spoken aloud in the community, or meditated on in silence, **prayer engages multiple areas of the brain**: regions responsible for language, attention, empathy, emotion, and self-awareness. In short, prayer is not passive. It is **a full-brain, full-body spiritual act**—one that forms us over time.

3.1 Types of Prayer and Brain Activation

Not all prayer looks—or feels—the same. Different types of prayer engage the brain differently:

- **Contemplative prayer** (meditative, wordless, or repetitive prayer like centering prayer or breath prayer) increases activity in the **prefrontal cortex** (focused attention) and **anterior cingulate cortex** (emotional regulation), while reducing activity in the **parietal lobe**, which orients the self in space. This reduction is associated with a **loss of ego boundaries** and a heightened sense of union with God—what mystics often describe as feeling "one" with the divine.

- **Intercessory prayer** (praying on behalf of others) activates the **empathy networks** in the brain—particularly the **mirror neuron system** and **temporoparietal junction**, areas involved in putting yourself in someone else's shoes. It also lights up regions tied to **social bonding** and **moral reasoning**.

fMRI studies from researchers like Dr. Andrew Newberg have shown that people in active prayer show:

- Enhanced focus and cognitive clarity
- Emotional balance
- Decreased anxiety and stress-related brain activity
- A shift from self-centered awareness to **God-centered presence**

What is remarkable is that the **content of the prayer matters less than the posture**. Whether the words are formal or spontaneous, it is the intention and sustained focus that rewires the brain.

3.2 Prayer, Stress, and the Parasympathetic System

In a world saturated with noise, anxiety, and overexposure, prayer can feel like a radical act of surrender—and it has **physiological consequences**.

One of the most well-documented effects of consistent prayer is **stress reduction**. Specifically:

- **Cortisol** (the body's primary stress hormone) **decreases** during and after prayer
- **GABA** (a calming neurotransmitter) **increases**, promoting a sense of peace and mental clarity
- **Heart rate** and **blood pressure** drop, especially in deep, contemplative prayer states
- The **parasympathetic nervous system**—responsible for rest, recovery,

and digestion—is activated, counteracting the chronic stress response of modern life

This aligns beautifully with Scripture:

> "Do not be anxious about anything, but in every situation, by prayer and petition, with thanksgiving, present your requests to God.
> And the peace of God, which transcends all understanding, will guard your hearts and your minds in Christ Jesus." — Philippians 4:6–7

This is not abstract encouragement. It is **neurological instruction**.

Regular prayer literally guards your brain against over-activation. It reshapes your baseline. People who engage in daily prayer report **higher resilience**, **improved emotional regulation**, and **greater recovery from trauma**. And these are not just feelings—they are reflected in **neural structure and chemical composition**.

Prayer is not a break from reality. It prepares your brain to re-enter reality with strength, presence, and peace.

3.3 Listening Prayer and Inner Attunement

We often think of prayer as speaking. But Scripture and spiritual tradition emphasize **listening** as a critical component. This kind of prayer—silent, open, receptive—is deeply transformative.

From a neuroscience perspective, listening prayer engages the **Default Mode Network (DMN)**, the system in the brain that activates during rest, self-reflection, and internal dialogue. The DMN is also where **imaginative and moral reasoning** happens—two essential components of spiritual discernment.

In listening prayer, you are not simply "spacing out." You are attuning. You are creating a space where your internal and spiritual world can align. You are opening the possibility that **God may speak—not audibly, but intu-**

itively—through impressions, scripture recall, imagery, or quiet conviction.

Hearing God in a noisy brain takes **training**. Modern life keeps the brain in **hyper-vigilant mode**—scrolling, reacting, and distracting. But stillness and attentiveness are like muscles. The more you practice them, the stronger they get. Over time, believers report:

- A heightened sense of peace and guidance
- Increased sensitivity to the Spirit's prompting
- A deeper awareness of God's presence throughout the day

Jesus often withdrew to quiet places to pray (Luke 5:16). In doing so, He modeled not just petition—but presence.

Reflection

> "Pray without ceasing." — 1 Thessalonians 5:17

This does not mean muttering words all day. It means cultivating a brain state that remains **aware of God's presence**, even in the middle of daily life.

What habits foster that kind of awareness?

- Breath prayers that regulate your nervous system
- Scripture meditation that anchors your thought loops
- Listening prayer that softens the noise of distraction
- Intercession that rewires your empathy circuits
- Gratitude that tilts your baseline toward hope

You were made for communion with God—not just emotionally or spiritually, but **neurologically**. Prayer is not a religious duty. It is **neural discipleship**.

Your brain is capable of becoming a sanctuary. But like all sanctuaries, it must be tended.

4

Chapter 4: Deconstruction — When Faith Meets Fracture

There is a moment many believers fear, avoid, or feel ashamed of—when the faith that once felt solid begins to crumble. Questions arise. Assumptions crack. God feels distant or even gone. What once felt like sacred ground now feels unstable. This moment has a name: **deconstruction**.

In recent years, the term has become widespread, and often misunderstood. Deconstruction is not always about abandoning belief. It is about **examining it**, pulling it apart to understand what was built on truth and what was shaped by fear, trauma, or cultural baggage. It is about facing the fracture honestly—and then deciding what, if anything, can be rebuilt.

Deconstruction is not just a spiritual journey. It is also a **neurological event**. Faith does not live in some abstract cloud; it is embedded in your brain—your neural networks, your memory centers, your emotional pathways. So when faith starts to break down, your brain **registers it as a threat.**

4.1 The Crisis of Faith: A Neurological and Spiritual Shock

Faith, once formed, becomes a **neural framework**. Beliefs live in the **prefrontal cortex** (where we reason), the **limbic system** (where we feel), and the **hippocampus** (where we store memory). When our beliefs are challenged—by life experience, trauma, new information, or internal tension—it creates **cognitive dissonance**: a stressful clash between two competing ideas.

> "If God is good, why did He let this happen?"
> "If this is the truth, why does it feel like a lie?"
> "If I leave this church, am I abandoning God—or finally finding Him?"

These internal conflicts light up the **anterior cingulate cortex**, a part of the brain involved in error detection and emotional conflict. At the same time, the **amygdala** (the fear center) may trigger feelings of anxiety, guilt, or even panic. The body experiences this clash not just as mental stress—but as a **threat.**

For those raised in rigid or authoritarian religious systems, the threat response can be even more intense. Leaving a belief—or even questioning it—may feel like betraying your family, your identity, your eternity.

This kind of spiritual disruption can look a lot like **grief**. In fact, neurologically, it often is. The brain processes it similarly to the loss of a loved one. Deconstruction can involve:

- Denial and bargaining ("Maybe I just need to pray more.")
- Anger and confusion ("How could they lie to me?")
- Numbness ("I don't know what I believe anymore.")
- Sadness and detachment ("God feels gone.")

And yet, this crisis—while deeply painful—can also be a **spiritual and neurological turning point**. Disillusionment, by definition, is the loss of an illusion. And the brain, while stressed by that loss, is also capable of **adapting and rebuilding**.

4.2 The Neuroscience of Unlearning

If belief is built through repetition, experience, and reinforcement, **unbelief** happens through **disruption**, **contradiction**, and **exposure**. This is how the brain unlearns.

One key process is called **synaptic pruning**. Just as the brain strengthens connections that are used regularly, it also eliminates those that are no longer useful or activated. In adolescence, for example, the brain undergoes massive pruning to streamline its function. But this can happen at any point in life, especially during times of stress or transformation.

When a person deconstructs their faith, the brain begins to **weaken the pathways** tied to those beliefs. This does not mean the person stops believing in God. It means the brain is **questioning the framework** it once used to define Him.

This is not rebellion. It is biology.

Jesus Himself challenged inherited frameworks. In *Matthew 15:6–9*, He rebuked the Pharisees for clinging to tradition at the expense of truth:

> "You nullify the word of God for the sake of your tradition... These people honor me with their lips, but their hearts are far from me."

Jesus was not afraid to confront religious systems that distorted God's heart. Deconstruction, when done honestly and humbly, is an act of faith—not defiance.

The brain may experience stress in this process, but it is also remarkably **resilient**. Neuroplasticity allows for **rebuilding**—a reconstructed faith, rooted in authenticity, stripped of fear, and reshaped around what is true and enduring.

4.3 Spiritual Abuse and the Brain

For many, deconstruction is not about theology—it is about **trauma**. Religious trauma is real. It leaves a mark not just on the heart, but on the **brain**.

Spiritual abuse occurs when faith is weaponized—when leaders use fear, control, shame, or manipulation to dominate others. It can take many forms:

- Being told questioning is rebellion
- Being silenced or shamed for doubt
- Experiencing exclusion or punishment for identity or conscience
- Being spiritually gaslit—told your trauma is not real because "God works all things for good"

These experiences activate the **trauma centers** of the brain. The **amygdala** becomes overactive. The **hippocampus** stores painful memories and scripts. The **prefrontal cortex**—responsible for rational thinking—often shuts down under emotional stress. The result is a body and brain that flinch at the thought of God, church, or Scripture.

This is not spiritual weakness. It is a neurological survival response.

Healing from spiritual trauma often requires **evidence-based interventions**:

- **Trauma-informed therapy** (EMDR, somatic experiencing, or narrative therapy)
- **Psycho-education** about religious trauma and the nervous system
- **Safe spiritual spaces** that honor autonomy, questions, and boundaries
- **Gradual reintegration** of healthy spiritual practices—on the individual's timeline

Theologically, it means rediscovering the God who does not coerce but heals. The Jesus who does not shame but welcomes. The Spirit who does not control but comforts.

Reflection

> "My God, my God, why have you forsaken me?" — Matthew 27:46

These are not the words of a heretic. They are the cry of Jesus Himself—the divine Son in a moment of excruciating spiritual pain.

That moment matters. Because it means even **God has felt God's absence**.

If Jesus could voice His anguish, you can too. If Jesus could question in agony, you are not less faithful for doing the same. Deconstruction is not the end of faith—it may be the **beginning of a more honest one**.

So ask yourself:

- What beliefs have I inherited that no longer align with truth or love?
- What neural patterns of shame or fear still influence how I see God?
- What needs to be unlearned—not to reject God, but to find Him more clearly?

This chapter is not the end of the story. But it must be faced.

You are not forsaken in your doubt. You are **held**, even when it feels like everything is falling apart.

5

Chapter 5: Reconstruction – Rebuilding a Faith That Fits the Brain and Soul

Deconstruction may feel like the end—but it is not. It is the painful but necessary act of clearing out what no longer fits so that something **truer** can take root. That next step—**reconstruction**—is less about returning to what was and more about building something new: a faith that is **integrated**, **embodied**, and **resilient**.

From a neuroscience perspective, this chapter is about **healing and reformation**—how new spiritual pathways are formed in the brain after old ones are dismantled. From a theological standpoint, it is about redemption—the Spirit's work in renewing the heart and mind (Romans 12:2) and making us new creations (2 Corinthians 5:17).

Faith, after fracture, can become stronger—not because it is rigid, but because it has been reforged in honesty, compassion, and truth.

5.1 Neurogenesis and Spiritual Renewal

One of the most hopeful truths in neuroscience is this: **your brain can grow.**

Even in adulthood, new neurons are born in a process called **neurogenesis**, especially in the **hippocampus**, the part of the brain associated with memory and emotional regulation. This means your mind is not locked in the past. It can be **rewired** toward peace, trust, and spiritual vitality.

Key practices that promote neurogenesis and align with spiritual renewal include:

- **Meditation** – especially contemplative prayer or breath-centered prayer. These practices strengthen the prefrontal cortex and reduce limbic system over-activity, allowing you to process emotions without being ruled by them.
- **Gratitude** – writing or speaking daily expressions of thanks literally shifts brain chemistry. Dopamine and serotonin levels increase. Neural patterns of pessimism weaken.
- **Community** – meaningful, vulnerable connection stimulates the release of oxytocin, a hormone that fosters trust and emotional safety. As iron sharpens iron (Proverbs 27:17), a healthy community reshapes the neural maps of attachment and belonging.

These are not just spiritual disciplines. They are **neurological interventions**, working in tandem with God's Spirit to rebuild the person from the inside out.

> "If anyone is in Christ, he is a new creation. The old has gone, the new is here!" — 2 Corinthians 5:17

This verse is not just theological—it is neurological. With every healed memory, every renewed habit, every reclaimed truth, a new creation is literally being formed in the brain.

5.2 Faith After Fundamentalism

For many, reconstruction involves leaving behind a **rigid or legalistic faith**—what might be called *fundamentalism*—in order to embrace a faith that can breathe. Not a diluted belief, but one that makes space for tension, nuance, and mystery.

Neurologically, rigid belief systems often reinforce **binary thinking**—black and white, us vs. them, saved vs. lost. This kind of thinking is processed through the **amygdala**, which deals with fear and quick categorization. It is efficient, but it is also emotionally reactive and easily manipulated.

Reconstruction involves engaging the **prefrontal cortex** and **anterior cingulate cortex**, areas of the brain responsible for **compassion, cognitive flexibility, and moral reasoning**. This shift moves us from reaction to reflection—from fear-based theology to **love-based faith**.

Reframed faith includes:

- A more generous view of God, one that is not threatened by doubt or difference
- A willingness to say "I don't know" without losing trust
- A theology that is deeply rooted but not tightly wound

Jesus Himself taught this way—offering paradoxes, parables, and mystery. He did not give formulas. He invited people into tension. Reconstruction does not mean throwing away doctrine; it means refining it until it reflects the God who is **both truth and grace** (John 1:14).

This kind of faith is **neurologically sustainable**—open, growing, and adaptive, not stuck in fear.

5.3 Practices That Rewire Belief

Reconstructing faith does not happen just through ideas. It happens through **practice**. What you do—physically, socially, spiritually—literally rewires your brain.

Embodied Liturgies and Ritual

Repetition forms habits. Habits form neural circuits. This is why ancient spiritual practices still matter today.

- **Liturgy**, far from being a dry tradition, offers consistent neurological reinforcement of theological truths. Repeating creeds, prayers, or acts of confession activates memory and identity circuits in the brain.
- **Rituals** like lighting candles, kneeling, taking communion, or lifting hands in worship engage the **motor cortex** and **sensory processing centers**, reinforcing belief through the body—not just the mind.

These embodied practices help anchor truth in times of uncertainty. They serve as neural "rebar," stabilizing a faith under reconstruction.

Journaling and Reflection

Writing out thoughts, prayers, and questions helps move ideas from the **limbic system** (emotional) to the **prefrontal cortex** (analytical), increasing clarity and reducing internal chaos. Journaling also increases **executive function**, helping believers identify what they believe and why.

Sacred Reading (Lectio Divina)

Lectio Divina is a slow, prayerful reading of Scripture that engages both the **intellectual and emotional brain**. It encourages a posture of listening rather than dissecting, reducing performance-based reading and inviting transformation.

Communal Processing

Reconstruction cannot happen in isolation. Safe spaces where questions are welcomed and testimonies are shared stimulate the **mirror neuron system**, reinforcing empathy, connection, and mutual growth. Spiritual growth is not just personal—it is communal, and the brain thrives on shared meaning-making.

Reflection

> "I will give you a new heart and put a new spirit in you... I will remove from you your heart of stone and give you a heart of flesh." — Ezekiel 36:26

This is not just poetry. It is a process. God is restoring your heart—and your brain—to softness, openness, and trust.

Ask yourself:

- What beliefs are worth rebuilding, and which ones are better left behind?
- What practices make your faith feel alive, embodied, and real?
- What is being reconstructed in your mind—and what is the Spirit forming through it?

You are not returning to who you were. You are becoming who you were always meant to be—renewed in mind, restored in soul, and rooted in grace.

Reconstruction is not a quick fix. It is a daily work of sacred neuroplasticity. It is the Spirit reshaping your brain to reflect the heart of God.

6

Chapter 6: Miracles, Mysticism, and the Brain

Religious experience does not always happen in quiet contemplation or structured theology. Sometimes, it explodes. Transcendent visions, mystical ecstasy, supernatural healings, or prophetic insight—these moments defy logic and exceed language.

And yet, they are reported across history, cultures, and religious traditions.

This chapter explores how **neuroscience** approaches the **mystical**—not to explain it away, but to understand **how the brain processes the extraordinary**. Because even if miracles transcend natural law, **our minds still experience them through physical mechanisms**. And that intersection—between spirit and synapse—is where awe lives.

6.1 The Neural Basis of Transcendence

Experiences of union with God, encounters with angels, or perceptions of timelessness have been documented in both religious texts and clinical studies. Neuroscience refers to these as **transcendent or non-ordinary states of consciousness**.

They can be triggered by:

- **Prayer or meditation**
- **Near-death experiences (NDEs)**
- **Psychedelic substances (psilocybin, DMT)**
- **Extreme fasting or sleep deprivation**
- **Spontaneous mystical encounters**

Neurologically, these states involve:

- **Deactivation of the parietal lobes**, which help define the boundaries of the self. This deactivation can result in feelings of oneness with God or the universe.
- **Increased activity in the prefrontal cortex** and **default mode network**, involved in memory recall and self-reflection.
- **Massive serotonin release**, associated with feelings of joy, love, and loss of ego.

In **2 Corinthians 12:2**, Paul describes a transcendent experience:

> "I know a man in Christ who fourteen years ago was caught up to the third heaven. Whether it was in the body or out of the body I do not know—God knows."

Paul's vision is neurologically consistent with what NDE survivors and mystics describe today: the blurring of physical boundaries, a sense of entering another dimension, and ineffable peace.

The **Qur'an** also references divine encounters and transcendence. In *Surah Al-Najm (53:13–18)*, the Prophet Muhammad is said to have seen "the greatest signs of his Lord" during his ascension (Mi'raj), an event rich with sensory detail, spiritual magnitude, and vision-like imagery.

These accounts suggest something universal about the human capacity to experience the divine in altered states—regardless of time, tradition, or theology.

6.2 Ecstatic States Across Faith Traditions

Beyond private mystical experiences, **collective ecstatic states** have played major roles in religious communities. Charismatic Christianity, Sufi Islam, Pentecostalism, Indigenous spiritualities, and Eastern traditions all feature experiences of:

- Speaking in tongues (glossolalia)
- Trance states
- Prophetic utterance
- Intense emotional release
- Physical healing

From a neuroscience perspective, these are not irrational—they are **altered neurological states** often associated with:

- **Increased dopamine** and **norepinephrine** release
- **Temporal lobe activity**, particularly on the right side (linked to emotion and religious intensity)
- Reduced activity in language centers during glossolalia (documented by Dr. Andrew Newberg), suggesting that **the person is not consciously generating speech**

Glossolalia, or speaking in tongues, is described in **Acts 2**, when the Spirit descends on the early church:

> "All of them were filled with the Holy Spirit and began to speak in other tongues as the Spirit enabled them." — Acts 2:4

Neuroscience has also experimented with **temporal lobe stimulation** using magnetic fields (as in Michael Persinger's "God Helmet"), which produced feelings of an unseen presence, awe, or overwhelming love. These experiences parallel accounts of divine encounter across faiths.

In **Sufism**, the mystical branch of Islam, ecstatic worship includes whirling, chanting (*dhikr*), and poetry that seeks divine union. Rumi wrote:

> "I lost myself in God and saw only God."

Brain scans of Sufi practitioners during *dhikr* reveal similar neural signatures to Christian contemplatives and Buddhist monks—suggesting that **the brain has a shared architecture for experiencing the sacred**, even when the language and doctrine differ.

6.3 Can Science Explain the Supernatural?

Here is the hard question: If neuroscience can map these experiences—pinpoint brain regions, neurotransmitters, and states of consciousness—does that mean the experiences are not real?

Not necessarily.

To say a mystical experience is "just the brain" is like saying music is "just vibrations." The fact that we can measure something does not mean we have exhausted its meaning.

Reductionism—the idea that everything spiritual can be explained by material processes—has its limits. Many scientists and theologians agree that **just because a spiritual experience has a neural correlate does not mean it is invalid**. It means the brain is the **instrument** through which we perceive the divine—not the source of it.

Consider awe. Whether standing at the edge of the Grand Canyon or weeping during worship, awe is a real emotional and neurological state. It makes people more generous, more open, more humble. Is it merely chemical—or is it a response to something real and greater than the self?

> "The fear [awe] of the Lord is the beginning of wisdom." — Proverbs 9:10
>
> "We will show them Our signs in the horizons and in themselves until it becomes clear to them that it is the truth." — Qur'an 41:53

Science gives us tools to **understand the experience**. Faith gives us a framework to **interpret the meaning**. Together, they do not eliminate mystery—they protect it from misuse.

Reflection

> "In the last days, God says, I will pour out my Spirit on all people. Your sons and daughters will prophesy, your young men will see visions, your old men will dream dreams." — Acts 2:17

So what part of the brain dreams prophetically? The same parts that imagine, remember, and feel. The same regions that hold your sense of self and your longing for the eternal. The parts that can be healed, rewired and made sensitive to the voice of God.

Mystical experience is not rare. It is deeply human. What matters is not how we explain it—but **how we respond to it**.

So ask yourself:

- When have I felt God most vividly—beyond words or logic?
- How do I hold space for mystery in a world of measurements?
- What does it mean that the same brain that fears also dreams?

Transcendence may touch your brain—but it does not begin or end there. You were made for the miraculous. And your brain—fearfully and wonderfully made—is part of that design.

7

Chapter 7: Worship and the Rhythms of the Brain

Worship is more than a religious act. It is a neural experience—a full-bodied expression that engages the brain, emotions, and body in synchronized praise. Whether through song, stillness, movement, or speech, **worship activates the deepest layers of human consciousness**, offering a powerful intersection between faith and neuroscience.

Across traditions—Christian, Islamic, Jewish, Hindu, and others—worship is not simply doctrine in motion. It is **embodied neural formation**. The patterns of worship shape the patterns of the mind. This chapter explores how.

7.1 Music, Emotion, and the Holy Spirit

Few things affect the brain like music. Neuroscientists have long known that music activates nearly every part of the brain—especially the **limbic system** (emotion), **motor cortex** (rhythm/movement), and **reward circuitry** (dopamine release).

When paired with spiritual language and intention, **music becomes more than emotional—it becomes transcendent**.

> "Whenever the spirit from God came on Saul, David would take up his harp and play. Then relief would come to Saul; he would feel better, and the evil spirit would leave him." — 1 Samuel 16:23

David's harp did not just soothe Saul's mind. It engaged his **nervous system**, altering his emotional state. Today, we understand this as a neurological response to music. But Scripture saw it first as an **anointed form of healing**.

Modern worship songs—whether whispered or shouted—release **dopamine**, the brain's pleasure chemical. Combined with emotional lyrics, repetition, and communal participation, worship becomes a neurological and spiritual high. But unlike secular highs, worship also engages **moral and relational centers**, anchoring the experience in connection with God and others.

In Islam, the **Adhan** (call to prayer) is often sung melodically, stirring deep emotion. The Qur'an itself is recited in rhythmic cadence, described not just as instruction but as a source of healing:

> "And We send down of the Qur'an that which is healing and mercy for the believers..." — Surah Al-Isra 17:82

Music in worship is not ornamental. It is **formational**, literally sculpting emotional and spiritual reality.

7.2 Embodied Worship: Movement and Memory

Worship is not just mental. It is **kinesthetic**—meaning the body plays a role in reinforcing spiritual truth. From kneeling in prayer to raising hands in surrender, physical posture **affects neural perception**.

Kinesthetic neuroscience shows that **movement and emotion are tightly linked**. Bowing, for example, decreases stress markers and increases humility and receptivity. Dancing increases serotonin and oxytocin. Repetitive rituals—when practiced mindfully—can create **multisensory memory**, embedding belief more deeply into both brain and body.

Biblical worship is full of embodied expression:

- *"Come, let us bow down in worship, let us kneel before the Lord our Maker." — Psalm 95:6*
- *"David, wearing a linen ephod, danced before the Lord with all his might." — 2 Samuel 6:14*

In Islam, **Salat (prayer)** includes a set of physical postures—standing, bowing, prostrating, and sitting—performed five times daily. This rhythm of embodied devotion shapes both spiritual consciousness and brain rhythm.

Studies on repetitive prayer movements show increased **parasympathetic nervous system activation**—meaning they **calm the brain and body**, increasing focus and lowering anxiety.

Movement in worship is not random. It is neural rehearsal for surrender, reverence, joy, and connection.

7.3 Communal Synchrony and Collective Consciousness

One of the most overlooked aspects of worship is its **social power**. Group worship—when people sing, speak, move, or pray in unison—creates what neuroscientists call **communal synchrony**.

During synchrony:

- **Oxytocin** (the bonding hormone) is released, increasing trust and emotional connection.
- **Heart rates, brain waves, and even breathing** can align across a group.
- The **mirror neuron system** is activated, increasing empathy and shared focus.

This shared experience fosters a sense of **belonging and unity**. It is why people leave corporate worship feeling more connected, not just to God—but to each other.

In Acts, the early church modeled this beautifully:

> "Every day they continued to meet together in the temple courts.

> They broke bread in their homes and ate together with glad and sincere hearts... And the Lord added to their number daily..." — Acts 2:46–47

In Islam, **Jumu'ah** (Friday congregational prayer) is central to communal worship. Rows of believers bow in unison, recite together, and end with greetings of peace. The result is **not only spiritual alignment—but neurological attunement**.

Communal worship does not just reflect unity. It creates it—at the level of the brain.

Reflection

> "Let everything that has breath praise the Lord." — Psalm 150:6

Worship is breath. Rhythm. Repetition. Emotion. Movement. Memory. Connection.

It is **how the brain trains for presence**—with God, with others, with self.

Ask yourself:

- What happens in my body when I worship?
- What memories are formed through sacred music, ritual, or movement?
- How does group worship shape not just my spirit, but my nervous system?

Worship is not escapism. It is embodiment. It is not just about **expressing love**—it is about **training the mind to return to it**.

You were made to worship. And your brain—designed by the God who breathes stars—knows how to respond.

8

Chapter 8: Sin, Shame, and Neurobiology

Sin. Guilt. Shame. These are not just theological terms—they are **neural experiences**. They shape how we think, relate, and see both God and ourselves. The spiritual weight of wrongdoing does not just impact the soul—it affects the **brain**.

This chapter explores how sin and shame function neurologically, and how grace—especially when received through forgiveness—can **rewire** the brain for healing and peace. Faith offers not just moral guidance, but **neurobiological relief** when guilt is processed healthily and mercy is embodied.

8.1 Guilt vs. Shame in the Brain

Though often used interchangeably, **guilt** and **shame** are very different—both spiritually and neurologically.

- **Guilt** says, "I did something wrong."
- **Shame** says, "There's something wrong with me."

Neurologically:

- **Guilt** activates the **prefrontal cortex**, associated with self-reflection and moral reasoning. Healthy guilt leads to conviction, responsibility, and repair.

- **Shame**, however, activates the **amygdala**, triggering a **threat response**. It floods the body with cortisol (the stress hormone), and can lead to withdrawal, self-isolation, and depression.

In *Genesis* 3, after Adam and Eve disobey God, their immediate reaction is not confession—it's **hiding**:

> "Then the eyes of both of them were opened... and they hid from the Lord God among the trees." — Genesis 3:7–8

Their response reflects the neurobiology of shame: the **flight** instinct. The belief that we are unacceptable leads to disconnection—from God, others, and self.

In the **Qur'an**, after Adam sins, he does not hide but **repents**. God responds with mercy:

> "Our Lord, we have wronged ourselves, and if You do not forgive us and have mercy upon us, we will surely be among the losers." — Surah Al-A'raf 7:23

The contrast is instructive: one response fuels isolation, the other invites restoration. Guilt can lead to repentance. But **toxic shame** creates neurological loops of fear, suppression, and distortion of God's character.

Understanding the difference is crucial—not only theologically, but for **emotional and spiritual healing**.

8.2 The Brain Under Condemnation

Living under a constant sense of condemnation alters brain function. It produces what psychologists call **trauma loops**—repeating cycles of negative thought patterns that reinforce fear, worthlessness, and separation from God.

These loops:

- Trigger the **amygdala**, keeping the brain in survival mode
- Shut down the **prefrontal cortex**, making rational thinking difficult
- Limit access to empathy, creativity, and spiritual openness
- Contribute to **religious OCD**, scrupulosity, or spiritual perfectionism

This is not conviction from the Spirit. It is **neurological suppression masquerading as holiness**.

Paul addresses this directly in *Romans 8:1*:

> "Therefore, there is now no condemnation for those who are in Christ Jesus."

This verse is not just a promise—it is a **neural reset**. It is the spiritual foundation for releasing the fear that drives shame and stepping into a state of grace that the brain can begin to **internalize**.

When this truth is believed and reinforced, it **rewires the brain**. The threat system deactivates. The **parasympathetic nervous system** (calming) engages. The person can think clearly, feel safely connected to God, and begin the process of spiritual and psychological integration.

8.3 Forgiveness and Neurochemical Freedom

One of the most neurologically transformative practices in any faith tradition is **forgiveness**.

Jesus makes it central to the spiritual life:

> "Lord, how many times shall I forgive my brother or sister who sins against me? Up to seven times?"
>
> Jesus answered, 'I tell you, not seven times, but seventy-seven times.'" — Matthew 18:21–22

Forgiveness is hard—but it is also **liberating**. Not only spiritually, but biochemically:

- Forgiveness increases **oxytocin**, enhancing empathy and connection
- It raises **serotonin** levels, improving mood and sleep
- It reduces **cortisol**, lowering anxiety and blood pressure
- It helps deactivate trauma pathways and reduces **amygdala overactivity**

Unforgiveness, on the other hand, keeps the brain in a state of **chronic stress**—tied to past pain and emotional reactivity.

The **Qur'an** also emphasizes forgiveness repeatedly, both divine and interpersonal:

> "Let them pardon and overlook. Would you not love for Allah to forgive you? And Allah is Forgiving and Merciful." — Surah An-Nur 24:22

Forgiveness is not pretending nothing happened. It is **releasing** the need to punish, handing the burden to God, and freeing the brain from **spiritual inflammation**.

Faith practices like confession, communal absolution, and inner healing prayer are not only biblically grounded—they are **neurologically restorative**.

Reflection

> "Then neither do I condemn you," Jesus declared. "Go now and leave your life of sin." — John 8:11

When the woman caught in adultery stood before Jesus, she likely expected shame. What she received was **mercy**.

This moment is not just moral. It is **neural**.

Jesus interrupts her shame response and reorients her identity—not by ignoring sin, but by reframing her in grace. This is the blueprint for neuro-spiritual healing: name the truth, receive mercy, and walk in freedom.

So ask yourself:

- Is the voice in my head one of conviction—or condemnation?
- What parts of my brain are still wired to expect punishment instead of grace?
- How might forgiveness—not just from God, but for others—free my nervous system?

Mercy is not soft theology. It is **hardwired hope**. When received sincerely, it changes everything—from brain chemistry to belief.

9

Chapter 9: Faith in the Face of Mental Illness

Mental illness is not a failure of faith. It is not a spiritual weakness, demonic possession, or lack of prayer. It is a complex interaction of biology, environment, trauma, and vulnerability—and millions of faithful people wrestle with it every day.

For centuries, religious communities either ignored mental illness or misinterpreted it. But today, a new conversation is emerging—one that integrates **faith and neuroscience**, spirituality and therapy. This chapter explores how mental health conditions like depression and anxiety show up in Scripture, in the brain, and the lives of believers.

Faith does not eliminate suffering—but it can offer profound tools for resilience, hope, and healing.

9.1 Depression and Spiritual Despair

Depression is not just sadness—it is a neurological state marked by changes in brain chemistry, energy levels, cognition, and emotional regulation. It often brings with it spiritual silence, isolation, and despair. And it has ancient roots—even in the stories of prophets.

In *1 Kings 19*, the prophet **Elijah** experiences what looks strikingly like clinical depression:

> "He came to a broom bush, sat down under it and prayed that he might die. 'I have had enough, Lord,' he said. 'Take my life; I am no better than my ancestors.'" — 1 Kings 19:4

Elijah had just experienced a miraculous victory over the prophets of Baal. But soon after, he crashes—emotionally exhausted, afraid, and ready to give up. His cry is raw, familiar to anyone who has struggled with depression: *"I've had enough."*

God's response is not rebuke—it is **restoration**:

- Elijah is fed (nutrition)
- Allowed to sleep (rest)
- Met with gentleness (no dramatic display, just a whisper)
- Given purpose again (mission and direction)

This pattern reflects a deep understanding of what depression requires: physical care, emotional space, and spiritual reconnection.

From a neuroscience lens, depression involves:

- **Low serotonin and dopamine** levels
- Overactivity in the **default mode network**, which fuels rumination
- Underactivity in the **prefrontal cortex**, reducing motivation and focus
- **HPA-axis dysregulation**, keeping the body in stress mode

Faith does not magically reverse these processes—but it offers a framework to **reintroduce hope**. Practices like prayer, scripture meditation, therapy, medication, and support groups all contribute to a more integrated recovery.

The **Qur'an** recognizes emotional pain too:

> "And do not grieve; indeed, Allah is with us." — Surah At-Tawbah 9:40

This divine presence in grief is echoed across traditions, reminding us that **spiritual despair does not disqualify us from divine companionship**.

9.2 Anxiety and Trust

Anxiety is the most common mental health issue globally. It includes generalized worry, panic attacks, and intrusive fear. Spiritually, anxiety often distorts our view of God—turning Him from a place of refuge into a source of pressure or disappointment.

But Scripture offers both **honest acknowledgment** and **calming practices**.

> "Even though I walk through the valley of the shadow of death, I will fear no evil, for You are with me..." — Psalm 23:4

Psalm 23 is one of the most anxiety-regulating passages in Scripture. It engages the **parasympathetic nervous system** through language of safety, stillness, and provision: green pastures, quiet waters, protection.

From a psychological standpoint, **faith-based Cognitive Behavioral Therapy (CBT)** combines:

- Identifying fear-based thought patterns
- Replacing them with truth-based alternatives
- Practicing **exposure therapy**—gradually facing the feared situation while anchored in trust

For example:

- *Fear*: "God won't protect me."
- *Truth*: "He restores my soul... He is with me."

Muslim traditions also ground anxiety in **trust (tawakkul)**:

> "Indeed, the believers are those who, when Allah is mentioned, their

> hearts become fearful, and when His verses are recited to them, it increases them in faith; and upon their Lord, they rely." — Surah Al-Anfal 8:2

Likewise, the **Torah** reminds Israel again and again to "fear not," reinforcing divine presence amid uncertainty (Isaiah 41:10, Deuteronomy 31:6).

Spiritual trust does not replace mental health tools—it strengthens them. It reminds the anxious brain that **not all fear is permanent—and not all suffering is solitary.**

9.3 Neuroscience of Healing and Resilience

Mental illness is not always cured, but healing and resilience **can be cultivated**—and both science and faith have something to offer.

Key neural resilience practices include:

Gratitude

- Daily reflection on what is good has been shown to increase **dopamine and serotonin**, reducing depressive symptoms and shifting the brain's bias away from negativity. In Scripture:

  > "Give thanks in all circumstances..." — 1 Thessalonians 5:18
  >
  > "If you are grateful, I will surely increase you [in favor]." — Qur'an 14:7

Community

- Isolation worsens mental illness. Healthy spiritual communities provide **emotional safety**, **oxytocin release**, and **relational healing**—especially when rooted in authenticity, not performance.

> "Two are better than one... If either of them falls, one can help the other up." — Ecclesiastes 4:9–10

Embodied spiritual practices

- Deep breathing in prayer, singing, and mindful scripture reading regulate the **nervous system** and lower cortisol. These practices create **neural space** for calm, focus, and hope.

Faith-Based Clinical Models

- **Christian integrative therapy** blends psychological insight with biblical truth
- **Pastoral counseling** grounded in trauma-informed care
- **Islamic psychology** (Ilm al-Nafs) emphasizes the harmony between soul (*nafs*), heart (*qalb*), and intellect (*'aql*), encouraging healing through both spiritual and mental alignment
- **Jewish pastoral psychology** centers on *teshuvah* (return), where healing is seen as a journey back to wholeness—with God and community

Together, these approaches honor both the **spiritual dignity** and **neural complexity** of the person.

Reflection

> "You keep him in perfect peace, whose mind is stayed on You, because he trusts in You." — Isaiah 26:3

The promise is not that peace will come from avoiding pain. It comes from **anchoring the mind**—bringing the spiraling, overactive brain back into rhythm with truth, presence, and trust.

So ask yourself:

- Where is my mental health affecting my view of God?
- What spiritual practices help calm my nervous system?
- What does it look like to seek healing—with both Scripture and science?

God is not afraid of your mind. He made it. And He is with you **in** the storm, not just after it.

10

Chapter 10: Identity, Imago Dei, and the Self-Aware Brain

To ask "Who am I?" is both a spiritual and neurological question. Human beings are the only creatures known to possess **self-awareness**, the ability to contemplate their existence, imagine their future, and construct a narrative identity. We do not just experience life—we tell stories about who we are within it.

This chapter explores how the **brain constructs identity**, and how Scripture speaks into that process. We will explore what it means to be made in the **Image of God (Imago Dei)** from a neurotheological lens—how empathy, embodiment, and connection shape the self, and how healing that self involves integrating both soul and brain.

10.1 The Narrative Self and Spiritual Identity

At the core of human consciousness is the **Default Mode Network (DMN)**—a system of brain regions that activate when we are not focused on external tasks. The DMN is responsible for:

- **Autobiographical memory**
- **Moral reflection**

- **Imagination and planning**
- **Story-making**—creating a coherent narrative of who we are and why we matter

Every person lives inside a story. That story is shaped by early experiences, relationships, trauma, culture, and belief. It answers:

- Am I loved?
- Am I enough?
- Do I belong?
- Do I have a purpose?

Scripture speaks directly into the formation of this **narrative self**.

> "For we are God's workmanship, created in Christ Jesus to do good works, which God prepared in advance for us to do." — Ephesians 2:10

The Greek word for *workmanship* is *poiema*—we are God's poem, His crafted narrative. Faith offers a redemptive storyline in which brokenness is not the end and identity is rooted in divine origin, not performance.

In the **Hebrew Bible**, identity is tied to calling and covenant:

> "I will take you as my own people, and I will be your God." — Exodus 6:7

In the **Qur'an**, identity is grounded in purpose and divine breath:

> "And when I have proportioned him and breathed into him of My [created] soul, then fall down to him in prostration." — Surah Sad 38:72

Across traditions, the human identity is seen as sacred, intentional, and

storied—not accidental. Neuroscience confirms that these stories when rooted in love and purpose, form **resilient neural pathways** that help us navigate life with meaning and hope.

10.2 Mirror Neurons and the Image of God

Humans are wired for **empathy**. When we observe another person experiencing pain, joy, or intention, specific neurons in our brain fire as if we were experiencing it ourselves. These are called **mirror neurons**—the neurological basis for compassion, imitation, and relational bonding.

Theologically, this mirrors something far deeper: the **relational nature of the divine image**.

> "Anyone who has seen me has seen the Father." — John 14:9

Jesus is described as the **perfect image of God** (Colossians 1:15), not only in divinity, but in relationality—He reflects the heart of God through perfect empathy, incarnation, and love.

Our capacity to reflect the image of God is not just cognitive—it is **interpersonal**. We see this throughout Scripture:

- *"Rejoice with those who rejoice, mourn with those who mourn." — Romans 12:15*
- *"Love your neighbor as yourself." — Leviticus 19:18*

In the **Torah**, God is described as **rachum v'chanun**—"compassionate and gracious," echoing the Hebrew root *rechem* (womb), a deeply embodied metaphor for empathy.

In the **Qur'an**, God's attributes include *Ar-Rahman* and *Ar-Raheem*—both derived from the same root, emphasizing divine mercy and closeness.

Neurobiologically, the more we practice empathy, the stronger our mirror neuron networks become. Worship, Scripture meditation, confession, forgiveness—these are not just spiritual disciplines, but **relational rewiring**

practices that make us more like the God whose image we bear.

10.3 Embodied Theology and Brain Integration

Modern Western faith has often been shaped by **dualism**—the idea that body and soul are separate and that the spiritual is somehow more important than the physical. But Scripture and neuroscience point to **integration**.

To be human is to be **embodied**. Every thought, prayer, emotion, or spiritual encounter happens **in a body, through the brain**.

Jesus affirmed embodiment by becoming human. He ate, wept, bled, touched, walked. In the resurrection, He did not discard His body—He redeemed it.

Neuroscience teaches us that our spiritual experiences are shaped by:

- **Gut-brain connection** (mood and decision-making)
- **Hormonal cycles** (stress, joy, peace)
- **Body posture and breath** (impacting prayer and meditation)
- **Trauma stored in muscle memory** (requiring somatic healing)

Spiritual growth happens best when we stop separating the soul from the body. Faith is more than belief—it is a lived, felt, experienced reality through neural and physical systems.

The **Tanakh** affirms embodiment from the beginning:

> "The Lord God formed man from the dust of the ground and breathed into his nostrils the breath of life." — Genesis 2:7

We are not just souls with bodies—we are **whole beings**, integrated by divine design.

Reflection

> "So God created mankind in his own image, in the image of God he created them; male and female he created them." — Genesis 1:27

You are not an accident. You are not just biology. But neither are you disembodied spirit. You are a **neurobiological image-bearer**—a mind, soul, and body integrated to reflect the nature of a relational, creative, and loving God.

So ask yourself:

- What narrative is shaping my identity—and does it align with truth?
- How am I reflecting the image of God in my empathy, my presence, and my relationships?
- What would it look like to love God with all my heart, soul, mind, and body?

You are more than your thoughts. You are more than your struggles. You are more than what others have told you. You are *Imago Dei*—crafted with divine intentionality and called to reflect that image in the world.

11

Chapter 11: Community, Church, and Collective Neural Health

Humans are wired for connection. Our brains are social organs, designed to thrive in relationships, not isolation. From attachment in infancy to shared worship in adulthood, our neural development depends on others. So it is no surprise that **faith itself is shaped, nurtured, and sustained in the community**.

The church—whether a small group, a global network, or a family of faith—has never just been a building. It is a **relational ecosystem** where spiritual formation meets neural formation.

In a time of increasing disconnection, digital saturation, and loneliness, this chapter explores how collective faith practices support **mental, emotional, and spiritual health**, and what neuroscience tells us about the power—and fragility—of community.

11.1 The Brain on Belonging

Belonging is not a luxury—it is a **biological need**. From birth, the brain is shaped by relational connections. **Attachment theory** teaches that early interactions with caregivers form internal working models of trust, identity, and safety—templates that affect how we relate to God and others for life.

Neuroscientifically, healthy community:

- Regulates the **amygdala** (reducing fear)
- Increases **oxytocin** (the bonding hormone)
- Builds **mirror neuron pathways** (empathy)
- Supports **dopaminergic systems** (motivation, joy)

The early church modeled this kind of neuro-relational safety:

> "They devoted themselves to the apostles' teaching and to fellowship, to the breaking of bread and to prayer... All the believers were together and had everything in common." — Acts 2:42, 44

This was not just spiritual intimacy—it was **neural coherence**. A group of people regularly sharing meals, stories, and worship were reinforcing **secure attachment** in both soul and brain.

> "Do not neglect meeting together, as some are in the habit of doing, but encouraging one another..." — Hebrews 10:25

Belonging is not just about attendance. It is about **mutual emotional regulation**, vulnerability, and shared story.

The **Torah** and **Tanakh** consistently ground identity in the community: Israel is "a people," not just individuals. Belonging is covenantal.

> "You shall be to Me a kingdom of priests and a holy nation." — Exodus 19:6

The **Qur'an** similarly emphasizes unity:

> "Indeed this, your religion, is one religion, and I am your Lord, so worship Me." — Surah Al-Anbiya 21:92

Faith is not fully lived in isolation. The brain was made for others—and so was the spirit.

11.2 Conflict, Reconciliation, and Neurochemistry

Where there is community, there is conflict. But Scripture and neuroscience both suggest that **how we handle conflict determines our emotional and spiritual health**—individually and collectively.

Unresolved relational wounds activate the **limbic system**, especially the **anterior cingulate cortex** (pain processing) and **amygdala** (threat detection). When group trust breaks down, the brain can enter a state of **hypervigilance**, reducing openness to God and others.

But healing and forgiveness trigger **opposite responses**:

- Increased **oxytocin** and **dopamine**
- Calming of stress responses
- Reconnection in the **ventromedial prefrontal cortex** (compassion and decision-making)

Jesus addresses relational rupture in *Matthew 18:15–17*, giving a simple but profound roadmap:

1. **Go to the person directly** (promotes safety and empathy)
2. **Bring witnesses if needed** (facilitates mediation)
3. **Engage community accountability** (preserves relational integrity)

This is not punitive—it is **trauma-informed spirituality**. Reconciliation, when done well, reactivates **neural pathways of trust** and restores **spiritual belonging**.

The **Qur'an** similarly teaches:

> "The believers are but brothers, so make settlement between your brothers. And fear Allah that you may receive mercy." — Surah

Al-Hujurat 49:10

The **Tanakh** offers practices of restitution (Leviticus 6) and sacred time set aside for release and forgiveness (Jubilee in Leviticus 25).

Neuroscience affirms what Scripture has always modeled: **healing does not just restore relationships—it rewires the brain**.

11.3 The Future of Church in a Disembodied World

As technology advances, church communities are being reshaped. Online services, digital discipleship, and even AI-generated sermons are becoming common. While these tools increase access, they also pose a challenge: **Can we form fully human faith in a disembodied world?**

The human brain was not built for persistent **digital engagement without embodiment**:

- Eye contact regulates the **nervous system**
- Touch and proximity release **oxytocin**
- Real-life rhythm fosters **emotional coherence**

An online church can teach, but it struggles to **form**. Without a shared presence, we risk turning worship into consumption and discipleship into content.

Faith formation requires:

- **Face-to-face vulnerability**
- **Embodied rituals** (e.g., communion, shared meals, baptism)
- **Multisensory memory** through touch, sound, movement, and presence

As AI becomes more integrated into spiritual spaces, believers must ask: **How do we remain deeply human?**

Scripture calls us into presence:

> "Where two or three are gathered in My name, there am I with them."

— Matthew 18:20

Community is not just logistical—it is **sacramental**. It reveals God through the presence of others.

The **Qur'an** cautions against superficial religion without relational depth:

> "Woe to those who pray but are heedless of their prayer—those who make show [of their deeds] and withhold simple assistance." — Surah Al-Ma'un 107:4–7

In a world of digital façades, the church must reclaim its role as a **healing presence**—a place where **embodied faith** meets **collective care**.

Reflection

> "Just as a body, though one, has many parts... so it is with Christ."
> — 1 Corinthians 12:12

Your brain is shaped by the people around you. Your sense of self, your resilience, your view of God—they are all influenced by the community you inhabit.

So ask yourself:

- Who are my people? Where do I feel spiritually and emotionally safe?
- What does it mean to be part of a body—not just theologically, but neurologically?
- How is my brain formed by presence, vulnerability, and shared worship?

You were never meant to heal, grow, or believe alone. You were made for communion—in every sense of the word.

12

Chapter 12: Toward a Theology of Consciousness

To ask what consciousness is—to wonder what the soul is, where it resides, and how it moves—is to stand at the edge of mystery. For millennia, faith traditions have spoken of **soul**, **spirit**, and **mind** as distinct yet intertwined. Today, neuroscience joins that conversation—not to resolve it, but to deepen it.

This chapter explores the **theological implications of consciousness**. It examines how we might speak of the soul in light of brain science, how freedom and sovereignty coexist in a wired brain, and what it could mean to believe in a world shaped increasingly by artificial intelligence and non-biological minds.

If we are made in the image of God, then consciousness itself is sacred terrain. To explore it is an act of worship.

12.1 What Is the Soul in Light of Neuroscience?

Neuroscience has advanced our understanding of cognition, memory, emotion, and self-awareness. But it cannot fully answer the oldest spiritual question: *What is the soul?*

There are three major theological perspectives:

- **Dualism** (most associated with Descartes and classical Christian theology) views the soul and body as separate entities. The soul is immaterial, eternal, and distinct from the brain.
- **Monism** (more common in some Eastern traditions and materialist science) views the self as entirely emergent from the body—consciousness is a product of the brain and ceases at death.
- **Integrative or non-reductive physicalism** (a growing view in Christian theology) holds that the soul is **embodied**—not reducible to biology, but not independent of it either. The brain is the vessel of consciousness, but the soul transcends its limits.

> "Love the Lord your God with all your heart, and with all your soul, and with all your strength, and with all your mind." — Luke 10:27

Jesus' command is deeply integrated: love involves **emotion, body, cognition, and spirit**. These are not compartments; they are dimensions of a whole.

In the **Torah**, the word *nephesh* (often translated as "soul") refers not to a ghostly spirit, but to the **living, breathing self**—a unified person, fully alive (Genesis 2:7).

The **Qur'an** speaks of the soul (*nafs*) as that which must be purified, elevated, or warned:

> "By the soul and He who proportioned it and inspired it [with discernment of] its wickedness and its righteousness, he has succeeded who purifies it." — Surah Ash-Shams 91:7–9

The soul, then, is not just "inside" us—it is **the totality of who we are**, in relation to the divine. Neuroscience maps the physical scaffolding of that experience, but it does not exhaust it. Consciousness is more than computation. It is where the divine meets the dust.

12.2 The Problem of Free Will and Divine Sovereignty

One of the deepest theological tensions is between **human freedom** and **God's control**. Add neuroscience into the mix—and things get even messier.

Research has shown that:

- Neural activity in decision-making regions often occurs **milliseconds before a person becomes aware of their choice**
- Habitual behavior is **largely unconscious**, governed by well-worn neural pathways
- Emotional trauma can impair decision-making and **distort volition**

This raises questions: *If my brain acts before I'm aware... am I truly free?*

Paul wrestled with this in *Romans* 7:

> "For I do not do the good I want to do, but the evil I do not want to do—this I keep on doing... Who will rescue me from this body of death?" — Romans 7:19, 24

This is not just a moral struggle—it is a **neurological conflict**. The tension between the **limbic system** (emotion, desire) and the **prefrontal cortex** (reason, will) reflects this battle between flesh and spirit.

The **Qur'an** balances divine sovereignty (*qadar*) and personal agency:

> "Indeed, Allah will not change the condition of a people until they change what is in themselves." — Surah Ar-Ra'd 13:11

We are shaped by biology, but not **defined** by it. Spiritual practices—prayer, fasting, confession, meditation—can **reshape neural pathways**, increasing our capacity for freedom and responsibility.

God's sovereignty is not threatened by our complexity. It includes it.

12.3 God and the Neural Future

As technology evolves, the boundaries of what it means to be human are shifting. Artificial intelligence, brain-machine interfaces, and digital consciousness raise unprecedented questions:

- Can a machine possess a soul?
- What makes human consciousness unique?
- What happens when faith intersects with **non-biological minds**?

Already, AI can simulate prayer, generate sermons, mimic empathy, and produce religious texts. But **is imitation the same as incarnation?** What separates a chatbot that quotes Scripture from a person who lives it?

> "The Word became flesh and dwelt among us..." — John 1:14

The Christian story hinges not on digital transmission, but **embodied presence**. God with skin, blood, neurons, and breath.

In the **Hebrew Bible**, prophets are often grounded in their physical world—eating scrolls, lying on their side, crying, bleeding. Revelation is never abstract. It is lived, felt, and embodied.

In the **Qur'an**, God addresses humanity through a Messenger—**not a machine**, but a living, breathing conduit of divine truth. The Prophet Muhammad, peace be upon him, embodied compassion, justice, and mercy—not as code, but as consciousness grounded in flesh.

As we step into a future of **augmented minds and digital consciousness**, the church must ask:

- What does spiritual formation look like in a world of neural implants?
- What is prayer in the presence of artificial sentience?
- Can a synthetic mind long for God?

The future may involve non-biological intelligence, but **faith must remain**

deeply human—rooted in love, struggle, worship, and the embodied image of God.

Reflection

> "Behold, I am making all things new." — Revelation 21:5

New does not always mean easy. It means re-creation. It means reformation. It means the merging of mystery and science, of Spirit and system, of dust and divinity.

So ask yourself:

- What does it mean to be a soul in a world of circuitry and code?
- How does divine renewal reshape your brain, your identity, and your future?
- In an age of rapid transformation, how will you remain **fully alive**—fully human, fully present to God?

Consciousness is a gift. It is the mirror through which we glimpse the divine. As neuroscience continues to map the mind, may we never lose the mystery of being image-bearers, beloved by the One who formed us—inside and out.

13

Chapter 13: Critics, Cautions, and the Case for Neurotheology

Neurotheology is a bold attempt to bridge sacred belief with scientific inquiry. But like any emerging field, it draws criticism—from both sides. Some theologians worry it reduces God to brainwaves. Some neuroscientists argue it overreaches the limits of empirical data. Others dismiss it as a trendy synthesis without solid footing.

This chapter addresses those critiques head-on—not to silence them, but to listen, learn, and refine. A mature neurotheology does not ignore criticism—it **grows through it**.

13.1 Is Neurotheology Reductive?

The Critique:

Many theologians argue that neurotheology reduces the sacred to the biological. They worry that if prayer, worship, or religious experience can be explained by brain activity, then it ceases to be **spiritual**. God becomes a neurological illusion.

This view often stems from a fear of **materialism**—the idea that everything, including consciousness and faith, can be explained without reference to anything divine.

The Response:

This critique misunderstands the aim of neurotheology. The field does not claim that brain activity **causes** God—it studies how human beings, **as embodied creatures**, engage with the divine. Just as the eye perceives light without *creating* it, the brain may be the organ through which we perceive God—without reducing God to a firing neuron.

> "The heavens declare the glory of God; the skies proclaim the work of His hands." — Psalm 19:1
>
> *Nature reflects the divine, but it is not the divine itself. Likewise, brain activity reflects spiritual experience—it does not counterfeit it.*

Neuroscientist Dr. Andrew Newberg emphasizes this point: "Studying the brain does not disprove God. It helps us understand how people experience God."

Even Scripture supports the use of **rational inquiry** into divine mysteries:

> "It is the glory of God to conceal a matter; to search out a matter is the glory of kings." — Proverbs 25:2

Understanding **how** we experience God does not negate **that** we experience Him. Knowledge of the system can deepen reverence for the Source.

13.2 Can We Trust Religious Experience?

The Critique:

Skeptics often claim that spiritual experiences—visions, tongues, transcendent states—are nothing more than **brain chemistry**. Hallucinations. Temporal lobe seizures. Meditative euphoria. These are real neurological events, but, critics say, they **do not prove anything spiritual is happening**.

This is sometimes called the **God-of-the-gaps fallacy in reverse**: if something can be explained biologically, it is dismissed theologically.

The Response:

Yes, spiritual experience is mediated through the brain. But so is **everything else**—love, reason, art, justice. The fact that these experiences correlate with brain activity does not make them illusions. It makes them **embodied**.

> "Taste and see that the Lord is good." — Psalm 34:8
>
> *This invitation to encounter God is sensory, not abstract. Spiritual life has always been* ***experiential*** *and* ***biological****.*

Religious experience across cultures and faiths shows remarkable **neurological consistency**. Studies using fMRI and SPECT scans confirm that deep prayer, glossolalia, meditation, and awe activate common brain regions. This does not disprove the experience—it **confirms its authenticity as a human reality**.

Even in the Qur'an, human experience of the divine is acknowledged as subjective and deeply felt:

> "We will show them Our signs in the horizons and within themselves until it becomes clear to them that it is the truth." — Surah Fussilat 41:53

Experience is not proof of theology—but it is **evidence of engagement** with the divine.

13.3 Is Neurotheology Scientifically Legitimate?

The Critique:

Some scientists view neurotheology with suspicion, accusing it of being too speculative, lacking standard methodology, or cherry-picking results that support religious ideas. There is concern that it leans too far into **confirmation bias**, especially when applied in apologetic contexts.

The Response:

These concerns are not without merit. Neurotheology is an **interdisciplinary field**, and like all such efforts, it faces challenges in establishing credibility. However, the field is growing rapidly, with peer-reviewed studies, university research centers (e.g., UPenn's Center for Spirituality and the Mind), and emerging clinical applications.

Key evidence-based contributions include:

- **Andrew Newberg's** neuroimaging work on prayer and meditation
- **Lisa Miller's** studies on spirituality and adolescent depression (published in *JAMA Psychiatry*)
- **Harold Koenig's** research linking religious involvement with mental and physical health outcomes
- Use of **fMRI**, EEG, and PET imaging to measure changes in neural activity during spiritual practices

The field is still evolving—but it is building on legitimate tools and expanding in rigor. Dismissing it outright is **anti-scientific**, just as uncritical acceptance would be **anti-theological**.

A mature neurotheology welcomes critique, demands ethical boundaries, and embraces complexity.

Reflection

> "Test everything; hold fast what is good." — 1 Thessalonians 5:21
> "And those who strive for Us—We will surely guide them to Our ways." — Surah Al-Ankabut 29:69

Criticism, when it is honest, is a gift. It sharpens ideas, clarifies motives, and strengthens what is true.

Neurotheology is not a finished doctrine. It is a developing dialogue. One that must remain accountable to Scripture, to science, and to lived human experience.

So ask yourself:

- Am I willing to explore the brain without losing the mystery of the soul?
- How can I engage in critique without becoming defensive?
- What does it mean to walk humbly—with both knowledge and wonder?

In the end, neurotheology will not rise or fall on the strength of an argument—but on the fruit it bears in the lives of those who seek to love God with heart, soul, **and mind**.

14

Chapter 14: Incorporating Neurotheology in Your Daily Walk, Worship, Service, and Quest for God

"You shall love the Lord your God with all your heart and with all your soul and with all your mind." — Matthew 22:37

"Be transformed by the renewing of your mind." — Romans 12:2

Neurotheology has given us a new lens. We have explored how spiritual life is deeply connected to the biological systems of memory, emotion, trauma, healing, and consciousness. But this knowledge is only powerful when it moves from theory to transformation.

This chapter is about **embodied discipleship**—learning to walk with God using all of what He created: heart, soul, strength, and *mind*. We now know that how we **live** our faith directly affects how our brains develop—and that how we **shape our brains** affects how we relate to God, others, and ourselves.

So what does it look like to live a **neurotheologically-informed spiritual life**? It begins in your daily walk, expands through worship, expresses itself in service, and matures in your quest for God.

14.1 Walking with God: Shaping the Mind Through Rhythm and Attention

> "Blessed is the one... whose delight is in the law of the Lord, and who meditates on his law day and night." — Psalm 1:1–2

Walking with God is not a poetic metaphor. It is a neural practice. The brain forms **habits through repetition**, **identity through narrative**, and **meaning through focused attention**. Each moment you consciously engage your mind in the presence of God, you are reinforcing neural pathways of trust, peace, and awareness.

🔬 *Neuroscience Insight:*

- The **prefrontal cortex**, responsible for attention and executive function, becomes more efficient when exposed to **repetitive spiritual disciplines** like daily prayer and Scripture meditation.
- The **Default Mode Network** (associated with self-referential thinking and anxiety) can be quieted through **intentional spiritual reflection**, shifting us toward God-consciousness.
- Studies in contemplative neuroscience show that those who engage in **daily spiritual practices** have lower levels of anxiety and depression, increased emotional regulation, and greater resilience.

📖 *Scriptural Grounding:*

- *Deuteronomy 6:6–9* calls for the constant remembering of God—while walking, lying down, and rising. This is **behavioral neuroplasticity** in the biblical tradition.
- *Luke 5:16* — Jesus withdrew often to quiet places. He showed that neural restoration is part of divine rhythm.

💡 *Practical Rhythms:*

- **Morning Focus Ritual**: Begin your day with 5 minutes of breath prayer and a short Scripture meditation. Engage your parasympathetic system before your day begins.
- **Digital Sabbath**: Designate time away from digital input to rest your overstimulated limbic system. Use this time for silence, journaling, or slow reading of sacred text.
- **Neural Anchoring**: Tie Scripture verses to locations (e.g., post Psalm 23 by your sink) to associate spiritual truth with daily tasks—this strengthens **environmental cueing** for devotion.

> "Verily in the remembrance of Allah do hearts find rest." — Qur'an 13:28

Walking with God is about choosing presence over distraction, rhythm over chaos, and alignment over autopilot. You are literally training your mind to dwell in the Spirit.

14.2 Worship as Neural Realignment and Sacred Integration

> "God is spirit, and his worshipers must worship in the Spirit and in truth." — John 4:24
> "Let the word of Christ dwell in you richly... with psalms, hymns, and spiritual songs." — Colossians 3:16

Worship is not only expression—it is **neural formation**. It is how the brain processes awe, gratitude, and meaning. Whether it is through music, movement, liturgy, or silence, worship realigns the brain toward **coherence**, **hope**, and **spiritual presence**.

🔬 *Neuroscience Insight:*

- fMRI studies show that **corporate worship** activates the **reward system**, increasing **dopamine** and reinforcing positive association with communal belonging.
- **Singing in groups** creates synchronized neural activity across participants—a phenomenon known as **communal entrainment**, which strengthens empathy and unity.
- Movement-based worship (e.g., dancing, lifting hands) activates the **motor cortex**, creating an **embodied memory** of spiritual truths.

📖 *Scriptural Grounding:*

- *1 Samuel 16:23* — David plays the harp and brings emotional and spiritual peace to Saul. Music literally calms a tormented mind.
- *Exodus 15:20* — Miriam leads women in song and dance in response to God's deliverance.
- *Surah 73:4* — "Recite the Qur'an in a slow, measured rhythm" — linking cadence with sacred memorization.

💡 *Forms of Neural Worship:*

- **Sensory worship**: Use candles, incense, or tactile symbols to engage multiple sensory systems.
- **Call and response**: Traditional in many worship settings, this technique reinforces memory and builds **left-right hemisphere integration**.
- **Silence and stillness**: Train the amygdala to stop over-firing by spending time in intentional silence (Psalm 46:10 — "Be still and know...").

Worship is not about performance. It is about realignment. It is about shaping the brain to trust the heart of God.

14.3 Serving as a Neurospiritual Practice of Embodied Compassion

> "Even the Son of Man did not come to be served, but to serve..." — Mark 10:45
> "Each of you should use whatever gift you have received to serve others..." — 1 Peter 4:10

Service is not just what we do—it is **who we become**. Compassion changes the brain. It releases chemicals that regulate stress, build social bonds, and create a sense of meaning and joy.

🔬 *Neuroscience Insight:*

- Acts of service trigger the release of **oxytocin**, the bonding hormone, and **serotonin**, which enhances mood and well-being.
- Volunteering has been shown to reduce **inflammation markers**, improve mental health, and even **increase lifespan**.
- The **insula**, part of the brain linked to empathy, lights up when we care for others. Regular compassion-based behavior reinforces these neural circuits.

📖 *Scriptural Grounding:*

- *Matthew 25:35–40* — Jesus teaches that serving "the least of these" is serving Him directly.
- *Leviticus 19:18* — The command to "love your neighbor as yourself" is both a moral and neural directive.
- *Surah Al-Insan 76:8* — "They give food in spite of love for it to the needy, the orphan, and the captive..."

💡 *Applied Neurotheology of Service:*

- **Trauma-informed ministry**: Serving others with an understanding of PTSD, anxiety, and neurological stress fosters true healing.
- **Compassion journaling**: Reflect on who you helped, how it made you feel, and how it shaped your understanding of God.
- **Cognitive empathy training**: Practice "imaginative intercession"—actively picturing others' lives while praying for them. This enhances mirror neuron activity and increases real-world compassion.

Service is not the overflow of excess energy. It is how the mind matures in the Spirit. It is not just an act of kindness—it is an act of **neural rewiring** for Christlikeness.

Reflection: A Whole-Brain Faith

> "You will seek me and find me when you seek me with all your heart." — Jeremiah 29:13
>
> "Let this mind be in you, which was also in Christ Jesus." — Philippians 2:5

You have walked through trauma and transcendence, doubt and desire, mystery and memory. Now it is time to integrate.

Your **daily rhythms**, your **worship**, your **service**, your **seeking**—all of it can be informed by what we now know about the human brain. And through it, we can more deeply reflect the One who made it.

Reflection Questions:

1. Which spiritual practices are forming your neural pathways right now? Are they shaping you toward peace or anxiety?
2. How can your brain-body connection become a more intentional part of your worship?
3. Who can you serve this week in a way that reflects both neuroscience and

sacred compassion?

4. How is your current lifestyle aligning—or misaligning—with your longing to know God more?

Neurotheology is not about novelty. It is about integration.

Not about proving God, but pursuing Him—with **your whole being**.

So walk it. Worship through it. Serve with it.

And keep seeking—because He is already near.

15

Conclusion

Loving God with All Your Mind

> "You shall love the Lord your God with all your heart, and with all your soul, and with all your might." — Deuteronomy 6:5 (Torah)
>
> "Love the Lord your God with all your heart and with all your soul and with all your mind." — Matthew 22:37 (New Testament)
>
> "Indeed, in the remembrance of Allah do hearts find rest." — Surah Ar-Ra'd 13:28 (Qur'an)

We have reached the end of this book—but the journey is only beginning.

We have explored the mysterious terrain of the **mind**, the **soul**, and the **neural networks** that bridge body and spirit. We have examined trauma and transcendence, deconstruction and healing, mysticism, and mental health. We have seen that **faith and neuroscience are not enemies** but partners in understanding the fullness of what it means to be human—and what it means to seek God.

This is not just about information. It is about **integration**.

Synthesizing Faith and Neuroscience

Throughout this book, we have seen how the spiritual life is not confined to rituals or beliefs. It is **etched into the brain**. Neural pathways respond to worship, prayer, Scripture, community, and forgiveness. Cognitive science and theological insight, far from canceling each other out, **complete one another**.

Faith answers the "why." Neuroscience explores the "how."

You were not given a brain to escape it in pursuit of the spiritual. You were given a brain **to love God with it**.

The God of Genesis who shaped humanity from dust also gave us neurons, hormones, and hemispheres. The God of the Psalms who knows our inward parts (Psalm 139) also knows our neural networks. The God of the Qur'an who is "closer than the jugular vein" (Surah Qaf 50:16) is not distant from the body—He **dwells within the design**.

Science can never replace faith. But it can serve it—by revealing the beauty of how we are made, the complexity of what we carry, and the miracle that **we are even capable of knowing God at all**.

Living as a Whole-Brained Believer

To love God with all your mind does not mean abandoning emotion. It does not mean reducing prayer to a chemical release. It means choosing to live as a **whole person**—not fragmented, not disembodied, not ashamed of how you are wired.

It means:

- **Renewing your neural pathways** through gratitude, meditation, and Scripture
- **Healing from trauma** through community, confession, and professional care
- **Practicing embodied worship**—movement, music, silence, stillness
- **Challenging fear-based theology** with truth, science, and love

- **Embracing complexity** instead of shrinking into certainty

A whole-brained believer is someone who is not afraid to ask hard questions because they know God is not fragile. It is someone who does not have to choose between therapy and theology, between clinical help and spiritual hope. It is someone who sees their mind not as a battlefield but as a sanctuary.

Continuing the Journey of Integration and Awe

This is not a "how-to" book with tidy answers. It is a **conversation starter**. A compass pointing toward a life where **faith and brain are aligned**, where neuroscience humbles us and theology lifts us.

The road ahead includes:

- **Expanding interfaith neurotheology**: Exploring how Jewish, Christian, Muslim, Buddhist, and Indigenous frameworks shape the neural-spiritual connection.
- **Bridging clinical neuroscience with spiritual formation**: Bringing pastors, psychologists, and neuroscientists into shared spaces of healing.
- **Developing trauma-informed churches**: Where forgiveness is balanced with accountability, and emotional safety is part of discipleship.
- **Ethical conversations about AI, consciousness, and post-human spirituality**: Asking not just what minds can do, but what they are for.

Neurotheology is still young—but its potential is vast. It invites us to hold wonder and wisdom together, to think rigorously, and worship fully. It challenges us to stop dividing sacred and scientific, and instead to live in **awe of how God meets us in both**.

The **future of neurotheology** is not just in labs or pulpits—it is in the lives of people who choose to live integrated, whole, and awake to God's presence in their bodies, brains, and communities.

> "He has shown you, O mortal, what is good. And what does the Lord

> require of you? To act justly and to love mercy and to walk humbly with your God." — Micah 6:8 (Hebrew Bible)
>
> "Whoever purifies their soul has succeeded." — Surah Ash-Shams 91:9 (Qur'an)
>
> "Be transformed by the renewing of your mind." — Romans 12:2 (New Testament)

So here is the final question:

What does it mean for *you* to love God with all your mind?

It means curiosity is holy. Questions are welcome. And awe is the most reasonable response to being fearfully, wonderfully, and *neurobiologically* made.

This is not the end. It is a beginning. May your journey of integration continue—with courage, wisdom, and worship.

Epilogue

In a world that often asks us to choose between science and faith, this book has made a quiet but radical claim: **you do not have to.**

Your brain is not a threat to your spirituality. It is a partner in it.

To pray is to light up the brain's attention and compassion centers.

To worship is to release joy-inducing chemicals and form memory through music.

To deconstruct is to rewire. To forgive is to heal. To meditate on Scripture is to literally renew the mind.

This is not a metaphor. It is biology. It is faith. It is both.

As we move forward into an age of rapid change—artificial intelligence, neurological enhancement, digital isolation—we must remember that **our humanity is not disposable**. It is sacred. Our minds are not just data processors—they are spiritual instruments, designed for wonder, shaped by suffering, and invited into love.

May your pursuit of truth be both rigorous and reverent.

May you never stop asking good questions.

And may your mind become, more and more, a place where God is at home.

Afterword

If you have made it to this point, you are probably someone who cares deeply—about healing, about truth, about people, about God.

Whether you are teaching this in a classroom, facilitating a discussion in a small group, integrating it into counseling practice, or reading alone in search of peace, **this book was written for you**.

Neurotheology is still young. But the work is ancient: to know God, to understand the self, and to walk with others through the mystery of both.

This is more than a conversation about neurons and doctrine. It is a call to become fully present—to yourself, to your people, to the God who made your mind and wants to renew it.

So keep going. Lead others with humility. Ask better questions. Stay human. And remember:

You do not need to choose between being **rational** and being **spiritual**.

You were created to be both.

About the Author

Dr. Corbett, DrPH, is a nurse, writer, researcher, and spiritual formation practitioner with a strong interdisciplinary background that bridges **public health**, **biblical studies**, and **neuroscience**. He is a **Certified Health Education Specialist (CHES)**, a **Certified Holistic Health and Wellness Coach**, and holds advanced credentials in population health and spiritual care.

Dr. Corbett serves as the **Overseer of Universal Deliverance Praise & Worship Center** and is the **Founder of He Cares Training & Education Center**, where he equips leaders, congregations, and communities for integrated healing—body, mind, and spirit.

His work merges evidence-based science with Scripture, helping people understand how spiritual growth and brain function intersect. Whether he's teaching, mentoring, or creating educational resources, his passion is to help others live in alignment with divine design.

When not leading or writing, he enjoys **quiet mornings**, **flying drones**, and **lifelong learning**.

You can connect with me on:

- https://drcorbett.my.canva.site
- https://www.he-cares-training-education-center.org

www.ingramcontent.com/pod-product-compliance
Lightning Source LLC
LaVergne TN
LVHW022310200926
848481LV00004B/1274
* 9 7 9 8 2 3 0 3 3 7 9 2 8 *